4-Hour Work Day
BECOMING A MORE PRODUCTIVE AND SUCCESSFUL BUSINESS OWNER

BY JON ROBERT QUINN

Introduction

It's 11 a.m., and you're two hours into your shift. If you're fortunate, you'll get home by 5:30 or maybe even 6:00 p.m. Yet, as soon as you step through the door, your wife and children need your attention. All you want is a moment to breathe, but before you can even take off your shoes or set down your keys, you're asked to handle this and that. While you love your family and would do anything for them, you simply need a break. It's been years since you took a family vacation, and you've managed to save up $300 for a weekend getaway over Labor Day. Though this may not be the case for everyone, there are families out there living in similar circumstances, where even the smallest of breaks requires months of planning.

This morning, you woke up and put your family's needs before your own. You left for work, fought through traffic, and, because you were running late, you didn't even have time to grab your morning coffee. You rushed into work, and before you even reached your desk, people were already demanding your attention. Your entire day is spent serving others, yet at the end of the day, you're left feeling drained, with little energy left for yourself or those closest to you. The unfortunate reality is that this cycle will likely continue for years—perhaps even decades—until one day you retire, hoping that somehow, you'll have enough money, time, and energy to enjoy the fruits of your labor.

I recently had a conversation with a wise woman who shared an insightful perspective on life. I mentioned how I had finally learned to relax, something my friends and family had been encouraging me to do for years. For as long as I can remember, I've been a high-strung person, constantly with a lot on my mind. A few years ago, I was working countless hours, completely immersed in my own world. My wife and I now live in a high-rise apartment in downtown Sacramento, just across from the Capitol building. Recently, we invested in some beautiful patio furniture, added lighting, and now every evening, we sit together, talking and enjoying the vibrant energy of the city below. We can see for miles in all directions, and the view is breathtaking. There are no phones, no computers—just the two of us, relaxing in each other's company. It's become our sanctuary.

4-Hour Work Day

This wise woman told me that I was fortunate to have found this sense of peace at such a young age. She said that most men, particularly business owners, don't learn to relax until it's too late. She recounted the famous last words of Sam Walton, the founder of Walmart, who, on his deathbed, said, "I blew it." Despite becoming one of the wealthiest men in the world, Walton worked himself to the point of exhaustion, never taking the time to truly enjoy life. Is this the kind of life you want for yourself? It certainly isn't the kind I want.

This book isn't about being lazy or neglecting your responsibilities. There's always work to be done. Instead, it's about finding balance—learning how to manage your business while also making time to enjoy life. It's about using your time wisely so that you can build a successful business and still have the time and energy to enjoy the things that matter most.

One of the biggest mistakes many business owners make is designing their businesses so they're always the ones in charge. This usually happens in service-based businesses where the owner can only make money when they're physically present. The problem isn't just that the business owner is in the driver's seat; the real issue is that they've structured the business in such a way that they *must* be there to generate income. If they get sick or injured, not only does the business suffer, but the impact on their household income could be devastating. Did you know that 40% of Americans don't have enough money in savings to cover a $400 emergency? That's a frightening statistic. If a business owner has to be open from 9 a.m. to 9 p.m., it's nearly impossible to work less than 12 hours a day. This grueling schedule affects your physical health, your family life, your relationships, and even your mental well-being. You've essentially become a slave to your business.

I've been there myself. Many years ago, I owned motorcycle shops, and I made the mistake of opening one in a mall. I was required to be there when the mall opened and stay until it closed. Those were long, exhausting days. On top of that, if I needed to file paperwork with the city, I had to hire someone to watch the shop, which created even more paperwork. There were days when I had to leave the shop unattended just to avoid fines from the mall management. Most people don't understand the reality of building a profitable and sustainable business.

Recently, I've decided to reopen my original store, but this time, I'm in a position where I can pursue building motorcycles as a hobby rather than as a job. I'm taking all the lessons I learned from my previous mistakes and applying them to create a more effective business model. With social media and access to suppliers in China, I no longer have to rely on expensive mainstream suppliers or spend enormous amounts on Google advertising.

In this book, we're going to explore how you can improve your business, find a better balance with your family life, spend more quality time with your loved ones, and live a healthier and more fulfilling life. What if you could work just four hours a day, five days a week? How would that change your life? What would it do for your relationships and your health? How much more would you enjoy life? Do you even have time for a hobby or passion? Most people don't, and that's something we're going to change.

It's time to take control, not just of your business, but of your life. Let's begin this journey together.

Rich Dad Poor Dad

If you read the book Rich Dad Poor Dad from Robert Kiyosaki, he talks about his rich dad, who was his best friend's dad and had a ton of money, owning many businesses, had all the toys in the world and had his freedom because he was rich. He also talks about his poor dad who was his real dad that was in education, had a mortgage and learned to play it safe but unfortunately died poor. Both were great men in their own respects, but one was rich and the other was poor. Personally, I don't like the words rich or poor because they have multiple meanings and are misleading to people who have different understandings of what those words mean. What he fails to explain is that most rich people are slaves to their business.

I have known many rich people over the years. I have also known many poor people. I used to be friends with the CEO of Raytheon. These are the folks that build our missiles for the Department of Defence. Will was a great guy with an incredible Ferrari collection. He also worked his ass off. When he retired several years ago, he moved on with his life and opened a winery in Napa's wine country. He figured it out while he was young enough that he could enjoy retirement. He worked hard. He earned a considerable fortune and he retired allowing himself to do something he loves to do. Unfortunately, there are many who do not follow this concept.

There's another gentlemen I knew named Josh. This man built a mortgage company in his 20s and sold it for a fortune in his 30s to a much larger mortgage company whom then sold to Elon Musk. This man has enough money to retire today and enjoy raising his family and travel with his wife. But he doesn't. Why? Because he loves mortgages? Or is it different? I'm not going bash the guy because he works hard or has a goal to be this or that, but he gets to work around 7am and gets home around 9pm and he does this six or seven days a week. I've seen him in public and he's tired and stressed and always in a rush but always seems to mention his new Porsche or whatever. What is he chasing? Who's the rich dad and the poor dad in this scenario? Both have fortunes. Both have the huge house, and I mean huge fucking houses. And both have some nice cars... Ferraris, Porsches, etc. But one is a slave to his business and the other is living and enjoying life.

4-Hour Work Day

Now let's flip the script. I have a client who's a business owner. He lives a modest home with furniture that isn't top notch and drives a nice car but not a high end car. He gets up in the morning for his daily yoga session, then often times takes trips into the foothills for a hike. He has a thriving business and works harder than most in his field. The difference is, he understands the balance. He's making a living and having fun while doing it. He's motivating, coaching and inspiring those around him and making an impact on the community. Adding him into the equation of the two men I mentioned earlier, who's the rich dad and poor dad now in this scenario? This gentleman here, Mike has a considerably smaller fortune than Josh and Will, but has the freedom of living a healthy, happy and prosperous life.

Josh is a slave. No matter how you look at it, he's a slave. Is that what you want? Do you want to have tons of money but nobody around you to enjoy it with? Do you always want to be chasing something and never finding satisfaction in anything because you're always chasing? I have been down that road and I can honestly say that it is a miserable way to live. Will worked hard, had a plan and retired young enough that he is living and enjoying life. Mike is still young, late 40s to early 50s and is making an impact on people's lives while continuing to build his wealth and create opportunities for those around him. In these three scenarios, I would have to say our rich dads are Will and Mike. Where do you stand? What do you want in life? How are you going to get there?

Working Smarter

Nothing irritates me more than having to do something more than once. My father always told me that it's quicker to do something right the first time than having to go back and do it again. Yet, so many people continue to half ass their way through life. Imagine getting up in the morning and going to work and doing the same thing over and over for years and years and never advancing or moving life forward. Me personally? I have my life so dialled that people are blown away I can accomplish as much as I do knowing that I take a nap almost every single day. Why is this? Because I work smart. Also, I believe naps are very important for physical and mental health. I have talked about this in other books and being able to have an hour nap mid day allows me to think through decisions and rest my body.

When I write a book like this one, I sell copies of the book for the rest of my life. People buy the books online, in stores, listen to audiobook and even watch the videos on YouTube. This equates to a considerable amount of residual income every month. I write the book one time and people buy it over and over again forever. Write another book and they buy that one too and then after you write five or ten books, a portion of your bills are paid every month. I also write and produce music and collect royalties on that. I build websites for small businesses and they have annual costs associated with that. And now I even own an indie TV network called JRQTV that produces better returns than any business that I have created prior. That being said, I still have to go to work like everybody else. My work is just a little different because my business requires less sitting in the seat in order to produce revenue. It's nice to wake up each morning to see how much money the business made while I was asleep. What's even more fun is going on vacation and coming home to more money in the bank than when I left for the vacation.

When you build a successful business, it needs to be profitable. One of the hardest parts of building a business is creating a model that makes money and can continue to make money during market trends and shifts. Getting into a bandwagon-type business like an MLM (Multi-level Marketing) will only leave you wanting more and almost instantly chasing money. Most people get into an MLM because they heard there is good money, only to find that once the money isn't arriving as fast as they would like, they bounce onto the next bandwagon. Unfortunately, the only ones making money is the company selling those memberships that you never did anything with.

Have you ever wondered why when an MLM opportunity presents itself in a community or region, the same people bounce from one to the other? They call you every six months to a year with the next big thing and after years and years of trying one thing and going to the next, they most often times end up in the same position they were in year after year. A few of them may get in on the ground floor and make a lot of money, but what happens when that model dries up? They end up right back where they started prior to joining that "opportunity".

I have always said that building a successful business stems from STP: Sustainability, Tenacity & Positioning.

Sustainability: How sustainable is your model or product? If there is a market shift, will you still be relevant or will operations be halted or dramatically affected? Is your business model recession proof? What happens if you're onto something big and you see your competition taking market share? These are things you really need to think about. When you look at businesses that were thriving prior to the Great Recession of 2007 and 2008, those business have either adapted and shifted their model or are completely out of business. The businesses thriving today during the Pandemic of 2020 are nothing like the businesses just ten years ago. Look at automobiles for instance. Tesla is king with their electric cars. Electric cars were few and far between with Hybrid just coming onto the scene. Companies like Amazon were in their infancy in 2007 and today, they are the largest company in the world. Even restaurants are different today with an array of food delivery companies that bring the food to you wherever you are at a moment's notice. If you wanted a steak at midnight just ten years ago, you were looking for a 24-hour grocery store and cooking it yourself. Now, you can pull up an app and in 45 minute, you've got your steak.

Tenacity: How much energy is needed to operate your business? Are you working yourself to death in order to make a profit or to get the business moving? When I sit back and look at my motorcycle business all those years ago, I look at all the mistakes I made. I had to be there sitting in the chair every moment that business was open, otherwise I was either fined by property management, or I wasn't making money. This is the biggest mistake business owners make. I see people that get up every day and go to work and then have a side hustle that requires them to be present and they are working 12, 14, even 16 hour days. This is crazy to me. All for what? To pay the bills? If they only understood that money isn't actually anything.

Positioning: What is your position in the market? Is your product or service needed? Is there a demand and is this product or service conducive to the times? Meaning, are you trying to sell cassette tapes of your speeches when nobody owns tape players anymore? Does this make sense? Also, getting into an industry when the industry is starting to die off can also be detrimental to the success of your business. A lot people spend so much time trying to perfect the cheese burger when McDonald's is still selling a lousy cheese burger and selling billions of them. The point is, get your product to market and make upgrades to your product as needed depending on the trends in the market. When a new iPhone comes out, it's never perfect. But the updates make it better and better until there's an even better iPhone.

If you have all three of these elements in your business, then chances are you will do fine, at least getting started. Then, it's time for you to systemise your business. Find ways to automate operations and systems so you can then let the business do what it needs to do. My business is virtually all profit. I have very little expenses to run my business and it doesn't require much time to actually get things done. Why? Because I put all of those pieces in place to build a model that gave me the life I wanted rather than become a slave to my business. Building an asset like this gives me the cash I need to build more assets. This is how people get rich. Let me explain in the next chapter.

A Slave to your Business

I have owned many businesses over the years and I have made a TON of mistakes. I have probably made every mistake you can make in business and today I sit here writing and thinking what mistakes I'm making now that in five years time, I will laugh at thinking how I could have ever done that. Unfortunately, we don't know what we don't know and the only way to learn is to learn from other's mistakes by reading books and hearing their stories or making the mistakes on our own and learning from them. Sadly, making the mistakes yourself can be very costly and time consuming.

There was a gentleman one year that was a business coach and gave me every reason why I needed to hire him to coach me in building my company. Shortly after I turned him down, he hold me that he was in hot water with the IRS because his "employees" were being given a 1099. Well, duh bro. If they are using your equipment in your office on your computers, they are employees and should be getting a w2 NOT a 1099. This is like business basics and this was a business coach. The point I'm making is, imagine the information he's feeding to these businesses. If he's making foolish mistakes like this, what bullshit is he feeding these businesses. Unfortunately, this happens all too often and kills businesses every day. No wonder the fail rate is so high. These poor business owners have no clue. They hire a "professional" and the professional doesn't have a clue what the hell is going on. It's sad.

4-Hour Work Day

My first business was a cellular phone business online working out of a small office I rented in some guy's house. This business left me in a heap of financial and legal trouble, but I was only 19 and have had plenty of time to clean up the mess and move on with my life as an entrepreneur. This also left me homeless for the first time. At 30, I did it again, except this time I was bankrupt and homeless. Today, I know what mistakes not to make and can recover quite quickly from little mishaps.

The phone business was high overhead with little margin that left me vulnerable in every mishap. My second business, the motorcycle shops were extremely high overhead with better margin but the expenses left me wide open for money problems and problems they became as I eventually lost everything. When I had the phone business, I was playing more than working. I was a kid with money burning a hole in my pocket and thought I was a badass because I had a business and fast car. I had no clue what the hell I was doing but teenagers typically don't. When I launched the motorcycle business, this is where I became a slave. I was working twelve, fifteen, even twenty hour days. I would order pizzas and just work through the day forgetting my surroundings. I was always playing catch up because I was overextended and didn't have cash reserves to do what I needed to do. We started falling behind on orders and eventually the cards came crashing down and that was it. I was working for essentially nothing and getting nowhere. I was however learning a lot about business and what not to do next time. These failures turn into wins real fast when you're experiencing new things and taking note of what to do better next time.

When I launched my current company in 2015, I knew so much about what not to do but still made a lot of mistakes as we were putting the pieces into place. One mistake I made was working myself to the bone. Again, I was working ten or more hours a day trying to make a buck so I could take this business to the next level. It's ok to work hard, but again, we have to work smart too. I used my training from the car and mortgage business and making cold calls all day then writing deals and prepping shows in the evening. There were times I would forget my wife was in the room and would tune everything out only to find that she'd been talking to me for ten minutes. Living like that is detrimental to both your health and your relationships with those around you. You're tired and irritable which then affects your client relationships which then make you work harder to retain your clients because you're pissing them off and losing them. Like I said, I have made a ton of mistakes.

4-Hour Work Day

It wasn't until a couple years ago that I really started to understand the balance. I heard somebody say that we only have about four good working hours in us each day and that got me thinking. When I sit back and look at the way sales organisations are run, these sales people slave to meet quotas, sales goals, bonuses, etc and the only person winning is usually the company owner. The ones who hurt the most are the families at home because mom or dad is always at work. It's just not fair and it's time to make a change.

4-Hour Work Days

When I sold cars, I was always ahead of the other sales people because I would work smarter rather than harder. The same thing happened when I was in the mortgage business. Though my tenure in those industries were short because it was supplemental income when I was building this company, I was still at the top the leaderboard because of my practices and discipline. My success then and today really stem from my discipline in myself and making sure I working to my standards. Working those jobs I was required to work eight hours a day but overtime was almost guaranteed. When a deal needed to be done, it had to be done. There were times my wife would come bring me dinner at midnight at the dealership while I was wrapping up a deal. However, when I was off work, I was still closing deals even though I was at the beach with my wife.

I have told this story in other books but I will explain it briefly here too so you understand the thought process and discipline I was referencing earlier. When I was in the car business, before I did anything each day, I would add all of our used car inventory to Craigslist with my phone number. I would then call all the dead deals, ie: people who didn't qualify prior to a car purchase and invite them back in for a second look. This instantly gave me an advantage. I would schedule appointments both for my working days as well as on my days off for other sales people to sell. Since I was the lead originator by setting the appointment, if there was a deal from my lead, I immediate got half the deal. So those other sales guys were closing deals for me on my days off or while I was working other deals. This is called making the system work for you and working smarter. The sales guys loved getting free deals but they were working for half the money. Shit, I set up the deal for them anyway. All they had to do was demo the client and write them up.

When I was in the mortgage business, I would look at who ever was #1 from the previous shift and take his number, then double it, then work backward and look at how many deals I would need per hour and per minute to hit MY goal. If I fell short, which was pretty much every day, I would still be #1 because I set higher expectations for myself. I was working the same eight hours, but I was making considerably more money because I was working smarter. The company had a $2000 bonus for the top performer. The entire 14 months I was at this company, I never missed my bonus. Sadly, there were sales people working an entire month to make what I made in the monthly bonus. Working just a little smarter pays off.

When I run my business today, I have the systems all pretty much automised. With JRQTV, my indie streaming TV network, I have traffic that is feeding in from YouTube. I get paid from YouTube monetisation for the content on there, which are businesses that have paid me to shoot their content. So yes, I am getting paid twice for that content. A lot of times my music from my music career is on the video so I collect the royalties from that as well. And of course all that traffic equates to book sales and other services my company provides. I can wake up in the morning and check numbers and see what happened overnight. From there, I can look at what appointments are on the calendar for the day. I try to sit with somebody new every day. This equates to new prospects and an increase of revenue.

Every day, I get onto Facebook and invite business owners to lunch at a local restaurant to talk business. We talk about their business. We talk about my business. We get a feel for our energy and see if it would be a good fit to work together. I may sit with four or five people before getting a sale, but let's looks at what this costs me. I have to eat anyway, so essentially I am only paying for their lunch. Let's say it's $20. I buy five lunches at $20, I've spent $100. I sell them a $500 to $1000 worth of marketing on my platform which essentially doesn't cost me anything because I built and own it and there you have it.

I can shoot three to five new clients a week taking maybe two hours for each shoot and edit. Then an hour lunch meeting and balance my accounts and I have worked a four day making anywhere between

$500 to $1000 a day. This isn't hypothetical and there are also days when I don't want to work at all. I woke up yesterday dedicating my day, my Thursday, to riding my Harley. Then today, Friday, I am relaxed and pushing hard to close a strong week to enjoy my weekend and start over again next week.

I do a lot of thinking these days. When I am working on a project like this book for instance, I may spend months thinking of content. Even when I write a music album, I have melodies, lyrics and concepts in my head. Then when I feel like I need to let it all out, it floods out of me with little effort and there are days I can sit there for only a few hours writing or working and after it all comes out, I feel like I accomplished and ready to take the rest of the day off. I may have only worked a few hours, but I created a new stream of income that will make me money for the rest of my life.

4-Hour Work Day

Excuses Kill Success

I know somebody who has a million excuses. We got pretty close for quite some time until I realised that she was becoming detrimental to my success. They say we are our circle of seven. The seven people we surround ourselves with is who we become. Imagine hanging out with one person who can't find a job, one person who uses the word "can't", one person that drinks too much, one person that does drugs, and another with bad credit. However, two of your friends are mildly successful. Where does that leave you? You're fitting into that crowd and accepting their lifestyle as your own, limiting your success.

Now flip the script and let's say that four of those people are real estate investors, one is a millionaire, one is an aspiring actor and another just graduated from a major university a bachelor's degree. Chances are, they will start to influence you to focus on your education, becoming a better and smarter person. See the point I'm making here?

This "friend" always had advice for me. She would say things like, "You need to learn how to deal with people" and "You need to be more patient" and "You're only further along in life because you're older than me." That is all bullshit. Those are excuses as to WHY YOU'RE FAILING. Let's wrap our heads around this. Chances are you're saying and doing the same things. We all do at moments in our life but making the habit of making excuses is what is keeping you from reaching your goals, or worse, creating goals. I catch myself making excuses for myself every once in a while and my wife will kindly remind me that I'm making excuses and this only motivates me to create action.

I wife will ask me to help with dinner dishes and in my head, I'm saying I don't want to, so I will say I'm busy. And in that moment, I am. I may have my laptop in my lap and getting work done. But what is really happening here is I am letting her down. After a while of making excuses as to why I can't help her, it will start to create tension in the relationship. Or worse, she trades me in for a younger model. Kidding aside, we don't want to let those down that are there for us, so quit making excuses. Had I just sat the computer down for ten minutes, she'd be happy and I would be getting my work wrapped up once the dishes were done.

People who make excuses for themselves unfortunately are the typical person in terms of daily actions. They get up in the morning and get ready for work. Then they get into their car and drive to a job they hate so they can work all day for somebody who is getting rich from their employees' hard work. That employer once had a dream to built a successful business and then hired you to run it, leveraging your talents to line their pockets. Then, you come home stressed from the job and get into bed and watch Netflix until you fall asleep, then repeating the process the next day. Isn't that the definition of insanity?

I am not bashing somebody for getting up and going to work every day. I commend them for being a productive member of society. However, this book isn't called How to Be a Productive Member of Society or How to Keep a Job. Sadly, that would be a book I should be reading rather than writing. This book is about taking your ideas, creating value for others and creating a path to success by working only

4-hour days. Working an 8-hour day for your employer is what we are trying to get you away from. It's time for you to become the employer.

Ok, so back to her claims. "You need to learn how to to deal with people." I do come across very brash and direct with people. I read bullshit very quickly and can size somebody up in a matter a seconds. Maybe that's a talent or a curse. I am not sure. But either way, I don't waste my time with people. When I ask a simple question, I expect a simple answer. When I ask a simple question and you're evasive or wasting my time with an answer, I will find the answer elsewhere and move on. I will also rip a clients face off if they hire me to help them and then feed me excuses. They either want to grow and change or they don't. I don't work with children, I work with adults. And, these adults are business owners. Therefore, there should be a need to want to be better and if they are giving me indicators that they don't want to grow, I will send them on their way.

Babysitting adults only hurts your brand and reputation. Let's say you're sitting down with a very reputable real estate developer and they want to hire you and your references are only the shittiest businesses in town. It looks like you're a shitty business too. Remember your circle of seven. You are who you surround yourself with. If you work with top quality clients, you'll be considered top quality too. If you work with shit clients, you'll be seen as shit.

Her second claim. "You need to be more patient." This kind of goes hand in hand with the previous statement but has some caveats. When I walk into a restaurant and there isn't a host and I stand there for five minutes with nobody greeting us, I will just take a seat myself, or simply leave. This all depends on how bad I want to eat at that restaurant.

4-Hour Work Day

When I am on the phone with a client and am helping them answer a question and they get a call and put me on hold, they have about one minute to get back to me or I will hang up. When I schedule a meeting with somebody and they cancel five minutes before the meeting, they will not get a second meeting with me. Why? Because they have no respect for me and my time. If they were to have a meeting with the President, would they cancel last minute? No, I doubt it. They certainly wouldn't get another meeting. Why should I be any different? And the same goes for you. Why would you give them another shot? All you're doing at that point is telling them that you will take any business that comes your way and work with anybody and that makes you look desperate.

My business does better when I am a dick and set boundaries up front. Before I ever take their money, I will tell them that I will be hard on them, expect a lot from them and will not tolerate disrespect or excuses. This sets the boundaries up front. Keep in mind that if a client that is a pain in the ass before you take their money, they are a bigger pain the ass after you take their money. That is the last thing you want. You never want to resent your client. You won't give them the level of service they deserve and that only hurts your brand and reputation.

The irony about shitty clients is, your intuition tells you a lot. If you don't feel right about the client, don't bring them on. It will only bite you in the ass down the road. Give them their money and send them on their way. It's so funny, or sad depending on how you look at it. I will have a client I fire and I think to myself and ask my wife if maybe I could have been nicer to them and then six months later somebody comes to me asking if I experienced this or that about this person and then I realise that my intuition was spot on. Then a year later I see them working with the other four shitty clients I fired. All the deadweight I cut loose are all working together on their shitty business and failing together. It's quite sad. Their egos are so encompassed around themselves that they only attract like and weak-minded people and I am sure they are all sitting talking about how big of an asshole I am. Sadly, years later, they never grew and they are only a distant memory to me.

And for her last claim. "You're only further along because I am older." This is complete bullshit. Look at Mark Zuckerberg. This dude was in his twenties when he became a billionaire. I was a teenager when I failed my first business. I was homeless at twenty from a business failure. Then homeless again at thirty from another business failure. This person I am speaking of is only maybe seven years younger than me yet I have 22 years of business experience and she has none. She's still getting up for work every day and doing the same thing and after 13 years at her job, she is still saying maybe someday she will own a business. This is the type of person that will be 60 and still saying maybe someday I will get that business I wanted to get started and all those ideas she had 40 years ago won't matter anymore. Why? Because of STP. The model doesn't have sustainability because the model is antiquated. She doesn't have the tenacity anymore because she's old. And, the Position is no longer there because again, it's antiquated. And this folks, is why businesses and people fail. Because they are full of excuses.

Risks of Entrepreneurship

I have been at this a long long time and have seen it all it seems. I have had clients come and go, family come and go, friends come and go, relationships come and go, money come and go, and even businesses come and go. Most importantly though, ideas come and go. So, which ones do you act on and which ones do you react on? Just remember STP. This will keep you on track. I have used this for years and it never lets me down.

A lot of things will happen in your journey as an entrepreneur and just remember, if you're slinging products for an MLM, you're not an entrepreneur. You just found another job that pays you a 1099. It's quite simple. An entrepreneur has an idea, manifests that idea into a product or service, creates value and a need for that product or service and then creates a demand for that product or service. Here's a list of things you can expect throughout your journey as an entrepreneur. If it's in your blood, like it is with me, then it won't scare you. You'll simply read this and chuckle to yourself because you understand what I'm telling you. If you get mixed feelings about entrepreneurship after reading this, then finding a job is probably a better fit for you. Ready?

Reading: There will be A LOT of reading. You will be reading and studying all the time. Whether you need permits, or corporate documents, or lawyers or even just know-how on how-to do this or that, it requires you to study. You need to know your field and your market. When I opened my Ferrari Parts business all those years ago, I had to learn every model Ferrari, year by year, the story behind the car, why it was designed or created, the names of colours, the parts, what parts superseded from one model to another and even what one country offered or restricted from another country. Since the service manuals were in Italian because the cars are made in Italy, I had to learn basic Italian just to understand the parts needed for those cars. In your business, be prepared to read.

Problem Clients: We talked about this before with the mentality of MLM people. They bounce from one idea to another trying one thing and not giving it enough time to flourish and then bounce over to something else hoping for better results. Business owners do this with marketing too and then have a sour taste because they feel like they were ripped off.

They come to me for a website and talk bad about the guy down the street. We spend weeks if not months building their website and then six months later, they are building another website with another company and most likely bad mouthing me. Instead, had they just stuck with the original guy, their website would be converting but you can't work with people that think they know everything. They read an article or something this one time and have it in their heads that it works this way or that way when in reality, just sticking the course will get them the results they need.

Recently a client came to me for some video work. We start shooting and after the first video, they are asking why I pushed it on social media in the middle of the night. My answer was because we wanted to capture the people scrolling on their phones in the morning and it will be in their morning feed. She proceeded to tell me I was wrong. If she knew so much, then why was she hiring me? She's been at her business for about a year and I own a TV network. You're going to run into people that tell you how to do your job. Personally, I think it's rude and disrespectful.

Slow Months: Slow months happen. You're going to have months that are amazing and feel like you're on top of the world, then other months that you're struggling to pay bills. You have to find that balance and only years of experience will get you this. You will start to understand trends in your industry and region and how to adapt to these ebbs and flows creating sustainability in your model.

When I first got into radio, I did know that April and May would be my slow months. You'd think that with tax time in April, business would be good because of refunds from the IRS. But with business owners, that's when we're paying taxes. Very rarely does a business get a return check from the IRS. They usually owe money, especially small business owners. You learn to adapt and plan.

Another thing I learned was to never pay my bills with my money. I always pay myself first and always find new money to pay that month's bills. You will always end up with the bills paid and you will always have play money set aside. I do my monthly budgets just about every day because money is constantly coming and going and when I am putting money away, every day the amount of money needed to cover monthly expenses change. The discipline changes your thinking and always leaves you in the black rather than in the red.

Multiple Fails: You're going to fail and you're going to make mistakes often. Sometimes they will be big mess ups that are embarrassing and bruise your ego and sometimes they are easy to recover from.

We all do it. My God, if you saw some of the mistakes I've made, you understand what I've been through. From opening stores too quickly and not having reserve cash to support the growth, to not paying Board of Equalisation and having my accounts levied to opening a C-Corp when I really needed an LLC. We all make silly mistakes but this is the only way we learn from them.

So many times I am with a small business owner over lunch or sitting there in their office and they are trying to figure out how to increase their revenue. They say they have tried everything but month over month they are getting the same results. I ask them a series of questions or sometimes just look around their office and immediately I see the problem. Small business owners don't realise that pretty much all of them make the same mistakes. It's usually an organisational issue, an issue with cash management, or even just STP.

There was one time, I was hired to increase business for a non-emergency transport company. I walk into their office and there were hundreds of sticky notes all over everything. They were on the walls, her desk, her computer monitor. They were everywhere. This was their organisational process. No matter what I told these people, I was wrong. Five years later, I am writing this book and they are no longer in business. There's your answer. Had they created a system to handle different aspects of their business, they would see growth but instead everything was written down and stuck onto everything. The problem with this model is things get overlooked for forgotten. I know exactly where my business stands. I know exactly how much money is coming in and out of my business. I know where my business is going. I even know where my client's businesses are going. Why? Because I'm organised. And guess what? No sticky notes.

Piles of Work: When you become a real entrepreneur, get ready for piles of work BUT it's how you handle that work that gives you the freedoms you want in life. Remember, this book is 4-Hour Work Day. So that means, get all your shit done in four hours and enjoy your life. There will be times where you work a long day or two. Hell, you may be down at your accountants office for three or more hours one day. That doesn't mean you only have an hour left to work that day. If you have shit that needs done, get it done so you can get back to your life.

Tony Robbins says it best. The best way to get organised in your business is to get the MOST IMPORTANT stuff done first. Usually when you have a pile of work to do, you get the easy stuff done first and then at the end of the day, you never got the important stuff done and the important stuff usually have time restrictions therefore leaving you handling these things as well. Instead, come into work and get the important shit done first. Get the things done that NEED done. Then when the important shit is done, you're usually on a roll and you can handle the easy shit next and before long, you're all done and can play the rest of the day.

Hire the appropriate people to handle things that don't pertain to your business. Hire an accountant or CPA. Hire sales people. Hire a cleaning company. Try to remove as much of the work as possible and create a system that essentially runs itself.

Lost Friends: This one I know all too well. You're going to notice a lot of things changing in your life as you become more successful. It's quite weird to be honest. First off, the people you thought were friends will no longer be friends. If this scares you, then just keep your job and be everybody's friend. I have to "fire" friends too because they drag me down or impair my success and true friends cheer you on instead of tell you everything you're doing wrong.

As you become more successful, your vocabulary changes. You find yourself getting smarter and your conversations change and your old party buddies that want to talk the good ol' days and what you used to do, no longer seem interesting to you. Depending on your field, your conversation changes to goals and dreams and your trip to Monaco or whatever. Here's an example. Your buddy Jim saved all year to go to the playoff games this year and you're sitting at the table listening to his story genuinely happy for him because he wanted something and worked hard for it and made it happen and at the end of the story, you genuinely congratulate him. And then he asks you what's been up. And you say, "you know, the same ol' stuff." He responds with, "still have the boat?" And your response is, "No, I sold it and used it as a down payment on a Ferrari" or something of the like. One of two things happen in this moment. He either is really happy for you and is like, "Oh man, no way. Dude, you've got to show me" or the other option is he feels inferior and his playoffs goal seems minute in comparison. Either way, you set your bar higher and made your goals happen and people should be happy for you. If Jim is genuinely happy for you and how brags to his friends that you have a Ferrari, then chances are he's a real friend. If Jim now starts to call you less and less or doesn't call at all or calls you a greedy asshole behind your back, then he doesn't deserve to be your friend.

Within that past couple years or so, I have found that people I have known for years just don't call me. I have one friend that sells cars where I used to sell cars years and years ago. Every time my wife and I would pass through town, we would stop and see him, give him a big hug and see how he was doing. He'd be in the middle of a deal and I'd ask if he needed anything or was hungry in which we would grab him some food and bring it back to him. We gave hugs and I wouldn't hear from him until next time we stopped to see him. I had a hunch one day that maybe these people I considered friends weren't actually friends at all. One day, I deleted all of the numbers from my phone. I then waited months for people to call me. I found that people I didn't even consider as friends were calling to see how I was and every single person with the exception on one, a guy from high school, never called me back. I then realised that all of those people weren't actually my friends.

4-Hour Work Day

Self Doubt: This one tears me up sometimes. As you become more successful as an entrepreneur you get high from your successes and achievements. You close a huge deal and feel like you're on top of the world and then a few days later, you hit a week long dry spell and you start to doubt yourself. Sometimes the doubt becomes depressing and this can be detrimental to your future deals. How? Well, nobody wants to do business with somebody who is desperate. If you seem desperate, then the client thinks you want to do business for the wrong reasons. If the client feels like you NEED the deal, then maybe everything you're telling him is bullshit. Instead, I just remain patient and if the client is stringing you along, just remember that if they are a pain in the ass before the deal, they will be a bigger pain in the ass after the deal.

One of the ways I have remained confident is by rewarding myself BIG when I win. If I score a large deal, I reward myself. If I fall into a dry spell, I reward myself again. Why? Well, it's psychology. When you're in the car business and you haven't sold a car all month, the desk man will always tell you to go buy a new car. All of a sudden, your spirits change and you're confident again and now you're closing deals and I can guarantee, you'll make more money than the cost of your new car if you apply yourself.

About a month ago I was in a slump. I was closing deals but they were maybe $200 to $500 deals and only a couple of those a week. I was making money but nothing like I wanted. I went to the Mont Blanc store and spend my rent money on a $900 Mont Blanc bag and a $500 Mont Blanc pen. My wife didn't freak out because she knew that my spirits would change and I would come home with larger deals the following week. The next week, I did $11,000 in business with $7,000 paid. A couple of the deals fell off which is normal in any business, but spending $1,400 changed my thinking and brought in larger and better deals. This week, I bought a Mont Blanc note pad for $75 and a new guitar for $700. This has me all fired up to wrap up this book and push hard for more new business this week.

A couple weeks ago, I purchased the 2008 Steve McQueen Mustang Bullitt because I could, not because I needed another car. I moved some of my finances around and paid off a couple credit cards and a business loan and made it happen because I knew my energy would bring in new business. The irony about my "friends" topic earlier is, as you're winning, you're welcoming better and more quality people into your life. Clients want to work with winners. Become a winner and you win even more.

4-Hour Work Day

The guy driving the modest car usually stays where he is unless he's in a specialty field where flashy shit is frowned upon. If you drive a Toyota and you're trying to inspire to become successful, chances are you're not going to inspire anybody. If you drove a Mercedes and all your clients were in a Toyota, then those are the people you end up inspiring. They may actually have more money than you, but because you're driving flashy shit, you look richer.

Burning Desire: For years, I have wondered what keeps me going. I don't have an answer for you other than the need to do something good in this world. The day I picked the guitar at 14, I never wanted to put it down. I played for six, even nine hours a day when I was younger. As I get older, there have been times where I didn't pick it up for months and then there it was back in my life when I needed to pour my heart out. When I failed my first business at

19, I was told I wasn't cut out for business and I believed that nonsense for about two years until I was thinking of all of these new business ideas and realised this is who I am. My entire life, I was called dumb because I failed out of school yet today, I'm a best-selling business author. I'm also an award-winning talk show host with radio shows all over the country. I'm even a recording artist and music producer and now even star in movies on the silver screen. What keeps me going? Honestly, I think it stems from my belief that we are only here on this planet to provide some sort of value to humanity. Whether that is growing grain, or enforcing laws, governing the people or in my case, using my talents to inspire those around me, we are all here to provide value to those around us.

You have to find your why. What drives you? If money drives you, then you're trying to grow your business for all the wrong reasons. You'll make more money as you become more valuable to those around you.

The Three Rules

There are 3 basic rules if you want to be successful. If you do not go after what you want, you will never get there. If you do not ask, the answer will always be no. If you do not step forward, you will remain in the same place. Let's discuss these:

If you do not go after what you want, you will never get there. You have to get off your ass if you want anything in life. When you see a pretty girl, do you let her walk away, or do you go up and introduce yourself? Well, if you're pathetic, you'll probably just let her walk away. If you're a guy reading this, you're thinking to yourself right now that this guy is pretty pathetic, but deep down you saw a girl so pretty you were too nervous or afraid of rejection so you walked away. If you're a woman reading this, I know for a fact that a cute guy at the bar was eying you one night, yet was too afraid to say hi so you let him walk away. And with good reason too.

This happens with business all the time. So many times, there's a killer opportunity and the idea that this could actually change your life comes to mind and immediately you're a deer in headlights and stop and run the other way. You're so comfortable failing that you impair your success. You're ok just getting by. What happens if I have so much money that I have to pay more in taxes? What happens if I have so much money that I have to hire people? What happens if I have so much money that my friends won't like me anymore or maybe I will attract gold diggers? Well, what happens if you so little money that you end up homeless or not being able to afford college for your kids or worse, not be able to afford the funeral for a loved one. Something like 40% of Americans cannot afford a $400 emergency if it happened. That is absolutely terrifying to me.

If you do not ask, the answer will always be no. How many times do you go to a hotel and ask for any specials or ask for free parking or even ask for an upgrade? You will be so surprised when you actually ASK for something. Every time I go to a restaurant, I politely ask for specials or discounts. When I go to hotels, I get all kinds of freebees by just asking. Business is no different. By simply asking for the sale, you will not only get closer to a deal, they will tell you their objections, or issues giving you the opportunity to work through them. You just have to ask.

Imagine going to the bar and you're sitting next to a pretty girl and you talk all night and never ask her name or even her phone number. You go home that night thinking to yourself that you just met this amazing person and you can't wait to see her again and next time you see her she's with her new boyfriend. Had you asked, you would be the new boyfriend. You'll only get out of life what you ask for.

If you do not step forward, you will remain in the same place. We talked about this one in the beginning of the book, but I will cover it again anyway. If you spend ten years at a job, not only are you making your boss rich, but you're keeping yourself poor. You have to take chances. Let's talk about Will Smith for a moment. I used him in an analogy from an earlier book, The Cold Call King, so I'll use him again here.

Will Smith in the 90s was a successful rapper with a multi-platinum selling debut album. His second album was a flop and left him broke. As he puts it, there's nothing worse than riding the bus when you're famous. His girlfriend at the time told him to go see Arsenio (Hall) and see if he had any work. He did and was told about a party later that evening. Will shows up for the party and Quincy Jones was there with an idea for a new show called The Fresh Prince.

Will was asked to audition and was told he had ten minutes to prepare. Will said he needed more time and they said ok, but the offer won't be here after tonight. Will went into a back room, got ready and auditioned for the role there at the party. Moments later, he met with lawyers in a limo parked outside to sign papers for his new show and rest is history.

In life, we are given ONE chance sometimes to become somebody. Sometimes you just have to take the leap of faith. When I was pitched to launch my first radio talk show, I had two weeks to figure my shit out. I had to come up with money, a lot of money which required me to find investors. I was broke. I had just left my mortgage job to focus all of my energy on my business and this opportunity fell into my lap. I knew it would change my life so I figured it out and made it happen. Now I'm rich. People hate me. A lot of people hate me. But more people love me than hate me and that's the point. You're reading this book and you'll formulate your own opinion of me but two things will happen, 1) I still got paid for this book 2) you'll walk away from this book thinking about something I said and it will change your life and your thinking forever. Whatever you want in life, get off your ass and go get it. It will not come to you. You have to go get it.

Getting into Radio

A lot of you may or may not know, I was at one point a national radio host on radio stations all over the country. This all started on accident. Or was it? I was a mortgage loan officer. I have talked about my story getting into mortgages in other books so I won't cover that here, but what I will cover is HOW I got into radio.

I had just been fired from my latest mortgage gig and was pretty happy about it. I was building Awepra.com now known as JRQTV and was ready to take this idea to the next level. When I was at Paramount Equity Mortgage, I would be building my platform on one screen and writing loans on the other screen. Most people were struggling to meet their numbers at work and I was not only #1 in the company in production, but I was also building my company at the same time.

I was now working at this shit hole mortgage company called Trinity Mortgage making half the money I was at Paramount Equity and was pretty sick of the bullshit there and one of the other agents was calling on my leads and I walked into the boss' office and told them to do something about this "clown that's stepping on my dick." I was fired that day. Good riddance.

Two weeks later I'm at Starbucks pitching advertising to somebody for Awepra.com and a gentleman walks over and tells me I should be building a radio show at a local station. Two things happened here. Opportunity #1 was him walking up to me and pitching me and the irony is, he was fired a week later because of poor performance. Apparently I was his only client in four months at the company. Opportunity #2 was that I took his offer and ran with it. This was exactly what I needed to take my career and company to the next level.

As we get older, our brains become a lot more comfortable with familiar patterns and routines. They become less agile and flexible. Neuroscience tells us that it becomes increasingly difficult to break out of existing mindsets. As a result, habits are formed which lead to rigid thinking.

When we look at the nature of habits, many of them are the result of a desire to avoid the repetition of a mistake. It's dumb to settle into a habit based on fear. A flexible mindset that thinks outside the box might look at a mistake as an opportunity to learn and not something to be avoided in the future. Flexible mindsets can seize opportunities because it always collects and processes new information.

Three weeks to the day after I met the gentleman from the radio station inside Starbucks, I launched The Good Life Show with Jon Robert Quinn on Money 105.5 fm. I was told by everybody that I would fail and would be out of business within six months. Ten months later, I was voted #1 FM radio in Sacramento. Shortly after, I launched shows in Seattle, Denver, and Miami as well. Within a couple years, I had over a dozen shows and was making insane money. I was making more money than I ever made at any other point of my life. And then I started getting stupid and bought everything whether I could afford it or not.

POOR

They say the acronym for POOR is Passing Over Opportunities Repeatedly. As I have grown as a business owner and mentor, I have coached hundreds of business owners and usually the ones that take my advice typically do pretty well and the ones that don't, well…. they usually fail.

The saying goes, "You can lead a horse to water, but you can't make them drink". This is so so true in business. Small business owners typically become business owners because they don't want to answer to bosses anymore and want to do their own thing and though the ideology is correct, they forget that their clients are their bosses now. Not only are their clients they boss, but there are protocols in business to ensure success. One of these protocols is taking opportunities that are presented to them. People are not dealt the same hand in life. They all have different starting points.

We are all born with different talents and abilities. However, we all have the choice to get better at what we do and, despite our starting point in life, we can often do something about it — to either get ahead, stay still, or slide backwards.

I prefer to view success in life as a choice. But I know many people who see things differently. Some people attribute the success of others to luck, circumstances, connections, and even family ties. These people are free to think that successful people are successful because of luck, but if that's how they want to view the world, then they haven't really explained why successful people are successful. They've only given an excuse for why they are not.

The bottom line is that successful people have made it because they had an opportunity and they made the most out of it. We all get at least one chance to make it big in life. Some people refuse the opportunity, some people don't recognise the opportunity, and some people *waste* the opportunity. So let's discuss what that means and how it relates to where you are in your life and what can you do to make things better.

I could be sitting at work right now in a cubicle waiting for my next break and texting my friends about what we're doing tonight and instead I am writing a book. This book will not only inspire others but it helps grow my brand and takes my company to another level and it also creates more residual income that will help me retire early. And as I continue to create more and more intellectual properties that generate revenue, I get richer and people will continue to tell me how lucky I am. I'm not lucky. I just got tired of working for the man and I also got tired of working for clients so I continue to create new products and I monetised my business and intellectual properties. Basically, I automised my business. THIS is how you get rich and you have the same opportunities I do.

A lot of people waste their opportunities in life by refusing to work hard. They get offered an opportunity and start working at it but they quickly get tired. They start thinking that their opportunity doesn't have much potential. They believe their opportunity will not lead to the future they desire. And they accordingly let go of that opportunity.

That usually happens when the opportunity comes and they're not prepared for it. They slacked off in the past. They didn't invest in themselves and their abilities. And now they don't have what it takes to take full advantage of the opportunities coming their way.

Some trivialise the opportunity. They think that working on their writing skills, communication skills and taking classes is not worthy of their time. They make fun of those that go to public speaking classes. They make fun of those that go to writing classes or marketing classes or business classes. They think such skills aren't necessary for success.

Average people tend to describe those who seize opportunities and succeed as "lucky." Luck has nothing to do with how successful entrepreneurs and business leaders do the right things to increase their probability of success. Successful people make their own luck. They ask this question: What can I do to change my situation? When they focus on the possibilities that lie before them instead of what they don't have, they seize control. This control creates success within the opportunity.

Quit Juggling

I have always had a lot of irons in the fire. At one point I had over fifty online websites selling products because my thought was to have quantity over quality. Well, where did that get me? Bankrupt. The lesson? Focus.

I must be honest — I'm talking to myself here. For most of my life, I've been moving from one opportunity to the other. That changed about ten years ago then I decided to only focus on growing JRQTV and incorporating everything I was currently working on and bringing all of my past projects into one place.

For many years, I had too many priorities and zero focus. It was time for me to rethink my opportunities. However, it's never a matter of finding opportunities. Everyone has opportunities. So it's not about how many opportunities you have, it's about how many opportunities you eliminate from your life and quit juggling. I see so many small business owners that want to be an overnight success and they are bouncing from one thing to another and become a jack of all trades. As I get older, I find myself doing less and less and that can be looked at two ways depending on your mindset. You could see it as I'm getting lazy or that I am getting more comfortable with my craft and putting quality into my work.

I had to make a choice. When you go to the circus, you see the juggler with four or five or even six balls and it sure is a sight to see. There comes a point where he's now got seven, then eight, then nine and when he drops one, he drops everything and in the business world, that's called a game over. I decided to only focus on my books, music, and JRQTV. Why? Because, they all complement each other and I realised it was time to focus on quality over quantity.

Something I get asked a lot is how I get so much work done. It always makes me smile when people ask me this as I often think that I could (and maybe should) be doing a lot more than I do. Something that I have been experimenting with this year though is not working on too many projects at once and not being afraid to say something will have to wait until next month. In fact I usually try to work on one main project at a time and schedule other things after that project has finished.

My day usually starts with me waking up naturally. I usually only schedule one appointment per day and usually after 11am so I can enjoy my morning. I am usually out of bed by 9am and walk the dog. Then I will take a shower and hop on the bike (Harley) and get Starbucks. I get back to the house in time to head to my meeting by 11am and then around 1pm, I am usually done for the day. I can spend the rest of day working on budgets, creating new products or thinking. I do more thinking than actual work these days. If I can film one new project a week and release one new intellectual property per month, such as a new book or new music, then I am staying productive and creating more wealth for myself. I do not do anything for my business that does not generate revenue.

So many small business owners create products and services and don't think about ROI (return on investment) and though creating intellectual properties only generate a couple of dollars or even just a few cents, when in volume, it creates generational wealth and in my opinion it's way better than real estate because there is virtually no risk. I can create music and get paid for the rest of my life from it. The same with books. I can write a book and it sells and the more I create, the more money I make for myself. This folks, is how people get rich.

Where to Start

So, you want to become an entrepreneur. Where do you start? You have an idea or provide a service that is needed in your community and are ready but you're still trapped by excuses.

I don't have the money. Chances are you DO have the money but you're using your money in the wrong areas. How much do you spend on Netflix or Amazon Prime Video or even Cable? Let's say you you shut those off and still need money. Then sell the damn TV and TV stand. Now you have money. How much do you spend when you go out for drinks? Quit drinking. This "friend" of mine I mentioned in the beginning of this book had every damn excuse in the book. She didn't have money or time but had money and time to go out drinking three nights a week. It's all about priorities folks.

I don't have time. Believe me, you have PLENTY of time. If you read my first book Tips to Increase Your Wealth, Health and Life, you can buy cheap sunglasses for next to nothing in China and sell them on the weekend at the flea markets. I made a TON of money out there. Some days, I came home with $800 after only a few hours selling in the hot sun. But people don't because they are lazy and then make up excuses as to why they cant do something and then give their friends and family lame ass excuses when they fall short and can't put food on the table or send their kids to college. It's bullshit and sadly, it's how I was raised. Maybe that's the motivation why I write these books, so people aren't making the same mistakes my parent made.

I don't know where to start. Start with buying books. I was sitting with a business owner this week that was bragging about how much money he had and asked me, "What do you think of the book Rich Dad Poor Dad?" I responded with, "It's the best damn business book ever written. It changed my entire way of thinking and my life and I wouldn't be who I am today, had I not read that book." His response was, "Oh." I'm thinking he was going to bash the book but he was just bragging about how much money he was making and how business was just so good. After our meeting and saying how he would prefer to pay me commission for revenue generated from my TV Network rather than buying ads, I walked out to my Steve McQueen Mustang Bullitt I bought from a week of business, and he walked out to an old Hyundai.

You have to start somewhere and he may be making money today, but in due time he will find new challenges and how he overcomes those challenges will determine how successful his business will become. Also, he will get smarter as a business owner and will talk less and listen more. There's nothing wrong with the guy. He just seemed green. He reminded me a lot of myself when I was starting out.

And as I get older and wiser, I tend to get along better with other, more refined business owners that have been around a long time. The conversations are different and more complex. As you grow, you'll know but you have to start somewhere.

It seems too hard. This is funny because hard is an understatement. Believe me, when you're getting started, it's almost impossible it seems. But when you overcome obstacle after obstacle, it gets easier and easier. It's like talking to girls. I was super shy when I was younger. I got so nervous I couldn't even function. My chest and stomach got a sick feeling even talking to a girl. Then I started dating.

Fast forward to my twenties and I always dated the ugly ones because they were easier to talk to because nobody was talking to them. Into my thirties and now I just don't give a shit. I get nervous talking to the super hot ones, but it becomes a high now because the girl that all the guys are looking at and are too shy to talk to, I just walk right up and introduce myself. Besides, I'm married so they aren't coming home with me... or are they?

You have to just put your fear behind you. Fear will cripple you. This is just you getting in your way and you telling yourself you will fail. But that's only because people that truly can't do something have been telling you THEY can't do it, so you can't too. But just because they can't doesn't mean you can and when you prove them wrong, they will either cheer you on or resent you and that's the real eye opener.

4-Hour Work Day

Get to Work

There is no magic potion or formula to get rich but wealth is accumulated over time. Just remember that rich quick, means broke quick. They never had to learn how to acquire and keep money, therefore don't know how to handle large amounts of money when they acquire it. When you're building your first business, you just have to make mistakes and learn and stay green.

Focus time every single day on your business. Be excited to come home after work and work on your business rather than watching TV. Rid yourself of distractions, ie: TV, bars, or other vices that keep you from reaching your full potential. Just this week I was asked if I drink. I told him I don't. He was surprised and asked why. I told him I like to keep my mind sharp. I am quick on my feet and always have an answer, even if it's a smart ass answer. Business is no different. I am always thinking of what's next.

I continue to organise and challenge myself and I never miss my mark. You'd be surprised how many people say they need my services and schedule an appointment only to cancel last minute and never reschedule. Years later, I will run into these people and they are doing the same thing they were but have a new idea and want to schedule an appointment with me. Being polite, I tell them to call me and we will sit down, but deep down I know they will never call. And, they very rarely do. So, if you want to be successful and start working 4-Hour Days, get organised, hold yourself accountable and discipline yourself for success and never fall short of your goal. It's your life. Make it happen.

www.ingramcontent.com/pod-product-compliance
Lightning Source LLC
Chambersburg PA
CBHW070810220526
45466CB00002B/616